STRIKING THE STONES

BOOKS BY DANIEL HOFFMAN

Striking the Stones
The City of Satisfactions
A Little Geste
An Armada of Thirty Whales

Barbarous Knowledge
Form and Fable in American Fiction
The Poetry of Stephen Crane
Paul Bunyan, Last of the Frontier Demigods

AS EDITOR:

American Poetry and Poetics
The Red Badge of Courage and Other Tales

Striking the Stones

Poems

by Daniel Hoffman

New York

OXFORD UNIVERSITY PRESS 1968

Library of Congress Catalogue Card Number: 68-18564

Some of the poems in this volume have appeared in *Antioch Review, Carleton Miscellany, College English, Columbia University Forum, Encounter, Hollins Critic, Hudson Review, The Nation, Partisan Review, Poetry* ('This Day,' 'Other Poems,' 'Testament,' 'When My Wiser Brother,' 'Entering Doorways,' 'In the Republic of the Troll King'), *Prairie Schooner, The Reporter, Sewanee Review, Shenandoah, Solstice, Transatlantic Review, Virginia Quarterly Review, Yale Review,* and the anthologies *American Poetry 1940–1967* (New American Library) and *New Poems 1967* (Hutchinson).

PRINTED IN THE UNITED STATES OF AMERICA

Again, MUSEBABY'S

Contents

STRIKING THE STONES

The Way It Is

They were waiting here to say
This is the way it is

This is the way

I came bawling into their domain
Of harsher light
Remembering a place
Of purer light and messages
Passed across a darkened transom
From that place
Remembering

They said this is the way it is
In this light this dust
This scuffle for the scraps, bad blood
Between unequals   You'll get wise
You can break
Your heart against stones here
Remembering.

Counsellors, betake your
Covenants of convenience
To a place of stones,

I
Must lift the shadow of each shadow
To find the dooryard
To that place.

This Day

Under what stone
Have you curled your snail's-horn while my blood
Ebbs down
To dead level
And feet crunch empty shells?

Dullard imagination, hiding
Your ecstasies from me,
Your curious tongue

Silenced,
Dry,

—I'll get by
In the light of this
Evacuated day,
I'll pick flat stones to scale
On the dead
Flatness
Of the sea

Until the one that hides you looses
Rings in rings
Spreading wider, nearer,
Long wet tongues to lick and lick
The silence of the shore.

There

Who'd go out there

On the black, humped
Slithering snarl of the sea

Past splintered
Rock hulls

Of islands wrecked by wave

Unless drawn
Inward

By her nets of song?

Other Poems

Flow in the pulses
Of my blood
Reaching outward
Toward clouds pierced by plunging trees,

    Other poems
Emerge in black weather
Under mercury arc-lamps where
Guards and mechanicians stalk
In tiled tunnels

Under the river
The cortège rolls

The current bearing
                  crates and rinds
Toward salt purification
                  of the sea

Blood
      tastes as salty
As the spume
Flecks on the wind veer

    Gulls dip and slash the wind
Sweep about our bed of shrouds
      Floating

And then I know
In the pauses of the weather and the dark
That love is a triumph
Of imagination,
      Wrestle
Of the river pouring
      Into the sea

Unmuzzled archangelic
Tongues
      Flare out
In the truth of trees.

Testament

A bare tree holds the fog in place.

It seeps out of irregularities
In gnarled twigs, those crevices
A nuthatch has picked clean

—One time there was a hill
Behind this tree
Dropped down,

A prospect of the tumbling
Breakers curled.

Fog has grown out of a tree.
I am the only
Thing moving

In this country.
No sky
Over no hill
Above no curved horizon,

The world contracts,

Interchange of codicils
Between one stem of taut limbs
In the damp halflight

Of this birdless day
And another.

In the Pitch of Night

White-throat beyond my window,
The sliver of your song
Pierces
The mist before the morning light
Shrivels the promises of night.

Your song
Changes nothing. The cold bay
Heaves and settles as before.
I cannot see you
In your cloudy tree.

Why do you thrust your silver knife
Into my silences? What undelivered
Letter will you open
Slitting the folded edges
Of my sleep?

It is darker
Before my open eyelids
Than in the clarity before
When I was hearing
From a burning tree

A sparrow sing.
I could all but see him in the blaze.
His unappeasable desire
Threaded across the sky
A testament of change,

Melting into song
Those pure resonances only
That echo
Without cease
Through discords dying all the day.

In Provence

A sky too hot for photographs,
A sky that bakes the toplids of the eyes,
A withered olivetree
That scratches at the crotches of the clouds
And on the rock
Among the sockets of the shadows
Lizards stop, and dart—

Here, amid the airs
Sweetened, pierced by wild
Thyme in heat, wild lavender,
It is the same
As under austere cranes that hoist
A frame of walls
Between us and the rigid sky

—The eye daring
Insupportable light
To find those slits in the familiar
Through which we peer,
Glimpsing then,
Or here, the only
Changelessness we'll know.

Domes

Boulevards receding
Point toward domes
That thrust their curves and tips against the sky.

City of lovely purposes,
Upholding balconies
Espaliered on walls
And windows
Reeling with cerulean light,

The nectar you have gulped
—No one was watching—
From night air, the dew, the morning light

Rises,
Bulging in the domes
You press against the heavens, thus
Nourishing your source

As our slight
Notions of a nobler
City and a perfect
Life, a faultless
Love arise
Toward theirs.

Instructions to a Medium, to be transmitted
to the shade of W. B. Yeats, the latter
having responded in a séance held on
13 June 1965, its hundredth birthday:

You were wrong about the way it happens,
You, unwinding your long hank of that old yarn
    Spun from our common dream since chaos first receded,
    As though a superannuated Druid were needed.

What looms now on that desert where the birds
Turn in their frenzy and scream uncomprehending?
    Not a cradled beast in whom divinity
    Could repossess the earth with fierce majesty;

We've seen the coming of a dispensation
Miniaturized in our set on the tabletop:
    Blazing from its pad, that rigid rocket
    No larger than the ballpoint pencil in my pocket

With its sophisticated systems for manoeuvre
And retrieval, the bloated astronauts within
    Plugged to cardiometers in weightless flight
    —Their radiant spirals crease our outer night.

No, you were wrong about the way it happens.
Our radar scorns all horoscopes. Where Phaedrus
    Tumbling past perfection fell toward birth,
    Junked satellites in orbit ring the earth

And circuitry has made the Tetragrammaton
As obsolescent as a daft diviner's rod.
    Yet you, a boy, knelt under Knocknarea
    Where the cragged mountain buffeted the sea

And knew a cave beside that desolate shore
Had been the gate through which Christ harrowed Hell.
        But what could knowledge of that sort be worth?
        Imagination would not rest; from that day forth

God-driven, you toiled through our long-darkening age
To do the work the gods require. In love, in rage,
        You wrote no verse but glorifies the soul.
        What's history, that we should be imprisoned

By some contention of the passing minute,
No sooner won than lost by those who win it?
        All action's but a strut between the wings.
        Our part you knew we each must play by heart,

By heart-mysteries that no invention changes
Though knowledge further than our wisdom ranges.
        'What matter though numb nightmare ride on top?'
        You knew there'd be a perturbation in the skies,

You knew, whatever fearful turn would come
By our contrivance, or immortal from the womb,
        Violence must break old tables of the law
        And old solemnities toward desecration draw,

But how conceive coherence with our power?
Old ghost, you seem to beckon from your tower—
        Moon-magic is the grammar of your speech,
        A cast of thought to keep within our reach

The tragic gaiety of the hero's heart
That blazes where the soul consumes in art
    All reality as faggots for its fire,
    Revealing the desired in the desire.

Then man, though prisoned in his mortal day,
In imagination dominates all time,
    Creates that past and future between which his way
    Unwinds with the fated freedom of a rhyme.

Words for Dr. Williams

Wouldst thou grace this land with song?
    Well, go yodel your head off.
But if it's poems you want, then take a town
    with mills and chimneys, oil
Slithering on the river toward the falls,
    grit in the air, a man
Just off the night shift turning, tired yet strong
    to watch the girl who hurries
Toward a timeclock step down from the bus—
    slim ankles, one,
Two, and click click click swings past. The sun
    glints on her raincoat. There's
Your muse and hero. Stick around this town
    where people speak American
And love is possible—Your stethoscope
    held to our arteries
In sickness and in health you found some places
    where our own poems grow.

A Visitation

Now why would a visitation from the Isles
Of the Blessèd come to Swarthmore,
Pa. 19081, a borough zoned
For single-family occupancy? No
Rocks of Renunciation on our
Assessors' rolls. Somewhere,
A consecrated shore
Ringed by dolmens where the wind speaks.
I listen to the hunger of the owl
Enclose the chipmunk in the quavering night,
I hear the plantain stretch its leaves to smother
Grass-shoots reaching toward the light.
The thick obituary of a lost day
Lies still on our writhing lawn.
And now the sky, black widow, pales
At the arrival of her new lover.
Between the thighs of trees old graves of sorrows
Open, and a fresh wind stirs.

Brotherly Love

[Saying, 'I am Alpha and Omega,
the first and the last:
and what thou seest, write in a book,
and send it . . . unto Philadelphia . . .']

I

. . . five , four , three , 2 , 1—
Now! Helicopters, disclose your secrets!
And smokestacks, for whom do your acrid plumes
Strut up the sky, then swirl and fall
In gritty exclamation points? I rub them
From my eyes, smarting
In the parking lot among unblinking
Headlights and the shrill rasp
Of meshed gears rattles the windows
In my head. Tonight the seasons
Stray as strangers where there is no seedtime
In the cinderblock. When on these plazas
Sacred groves appear we shall
Long since have snuffed the blowtorch
That consummates the raising
Of this busy city. See, already
Bulldozers like gross maenads herd together
For the rending of its bones.

II

Standing around
Waiting for something—
A rumble,

Maybe, or the bursting
Black blister of
Rage burnt white-hot by

A word, a laying
On of hands and then the first
Bottle crashes

Through the windshield
And the storefronts
Shatter

As the city
Writhes in seizure,
Its sores burning,

But their transistors only
Proclaim the mopping
Up in distant

Da Nang, pinned
To the wall by
Sniper fire

And here
The afternoon
Sweats where broken

Beerbottles
Glint darkly, waiting
For the action.

III

Smudge from a balky lighter
and a low–hulled, smoking tramp
blurs the docks. Down Market Street
the fierce moonlight of mercury lamps

sanitizes pavements Walt
Whitman used to walk.
Here Poe and Brockden Brown
were stalked by demons through the town

past the dormered, brickwork houses
of our Colonial century
(now lavishly restored
to Federal austerity)

where shoppers jostle. Wait! I'd join
you, seers of the soul's exile!
From Christ Church vaults the pigeons foul
our Signers seem to give no sign,

but over Wanamaker's lights
Billy Penn extends indulgent arms,
still beckoning the Welsh and Mennonites
to his green outlying farms,

stone blind. His mood
seems benign though slum-blocks sprawl,
blotches of hives, across Penn's Wood.
Beyond, bulldozers snarl;

behind his back high-rise
investments abruptly obtrude
on our only noble boulevard
proportioned to delight men's eyes.

No hour but is a rush hour, and where rushing?
We cram the days, but there's no use,
our history grows longer, longer.
It's life that's getting away from us

while the changing city seethes with being.
Our Founder's feet are stuck
to the cranium of a clock
whose four faces gaze on us unseeing.

On the Industrial Highway

Approaching the Walt
Whitman Bridge you pass
an affluent world—

a subculture of spouts,
nozzles, ducts, a host
of snakes and ladders

in nests and thickets
or by tribes, laying
dinosaur farts

against the sun.
I drive slowly through the
stink and gawk at

shapes that no
familiarity breeds,
a ghostless city

called 'gas works,' never
meant for death or living.
A pipe pulses

flame in secret
code on the gashed sky.
Here are things

whose archetypes
have not yet been dreamed.
There's no more perfect

duct than these
ducts, pipes, facts
burdened with nothing

anticipating
unhappencd memories,
visionary things.

Asylum

After the tour was over, we drove home
Past probing steeples of the radar screen
For Greater Philadelphia. The screams
Of jets bounced back from high walls of the sky;
Beyond the Industrial Highway, orange gloom
Hung over rows of intricate towers moored
In the river by the Navy Yard.
Upstream, the bleak spires of our city loomed,
But on that island we had come from
Sycamores arched across the water.
Peacocks, elegant in saunter, leaned
Cockaded heads in a rage toward us—they'd scream,
Scream us away. In the rhododendron
With mâchicoulis of Sears Roebuck picket fencing,
Purple battlements behind a vermilion drawbridge
Menaced the implausible Poconos.
Ten yards away, above the falls,
The good ship thwarts the current. Steady oars
Sweep long ripples as the gig
Glides nowhere on matched fours.
Imperial Marines lean back to pull
In everlasting fealty to their Admiral
The Emperor, who paces on the parapet.
Astern, a waterwheel is turning—what intricacies
Of crankshaft rig it to the dummy oarsmen!
—A classic therapy, they amusedly explain—
This is his life,
He's harmless in his kingdom.

Crop-Dusting

The mice rot in their tunnels in a field
Where phantom harvesters cut phantom grain.
A poisoned acre grows a poisoned yield.

Here skinny children stretch their hands in vain.
Their swollen bellies hurt, and are not healed.
A phantom blade has harvested their grain.

Night after night I see this land annealed
By draughts of fire and death that fall like rain.
One poisoned acre poisons all the field.

These are my crops. We harrow my domain.
The one who pays counts all for which he's billed.
A phantom harvester stacks phantom grain.

To own such wealth as this my heart I've steeled
And all but stilled the tumult in my brain.
My poisoned acre grows a poisoned yield.

Unable to be dispossessed by Cain,
In his accounts my civil tithes are sealed.
And how renounce the poisoning of this field,
Or be forgiven the reaping of its grain?

'What will they think of us the dead'

What will they think of us the dead
Who have reclaimed

Their maimed eyes their separate arms
The matched pairs

Of knees and ankles   scattered bits
And pieces of their private parts

The pure essence only
Of blood shunting

Through their veins their hearts
Their simplest thought possessing now

A luminescence
That shows our boldest speculations

Half shadow—
What will they think who know

The soul's appeasement of its first desire
The quench of pride

Satiation of the mind   the will
And power

An untranslatable
Incrimination in a disused tongue

—Will they remember
How we communicate in that lost tongue

How power and pride
Will not be satiate

How our will
Blacks out

The pure the intellectual light
How turns aside

The soul's desire from love   converts
The instruments of our delight

To engines that appall
And sends to crawl on minefields boys

Whose cares do they recall were theirs
Whose loves were their sole joys?

Shaking the President's Hand

Who'd be likely to forget
His brief squeeze by those brisk fingers,
The First Citizen's! The touch of kings
Was blessed, a gift to remedy
The King's Evil. Here
Where every man's a king,
What did I touch a President to cure?

The Peaceable Kingdom

[The Phi Beta Kappa Poem
Swarthmore College, 1964]

I

Now that we sponsor the extirpation of folklore,
    The growing scarcity of trees,
Bulldozers gouging roadbeds through the valleys,
    Traffic clogged where streams once flowed,
More people nourished by more Inplant Feeding,
    The disuse of Deer Crossing signs,
Proliferation of home-heliports,
    Attrition of the harvest-home
And slagheaps overshadowing the city,
    The mountain's heart quarried away,
Ingurgitation of knowledge by computers
    Whose feedback gives for wisdom facts
Elicited by robots or commuters
    Grown unhandy with real things
From much manipulation of abstractions,
    The seasons seldom touching them,
Not even benign falls of snow disguising
    A land it will be harder to love;

29

Where Opulence, demotic *arriviste,*
        Counts his costly toys like beads
While Penury gnaws knuckled fists, her brawling
        Brood of brats picking through trash,
The sullen disinherited and darker
        Faces massing in the square
As though impatient with their ill provision
        Despite the auspex of Dow Jones
That proves the National Gross Product growing,
        The deserts paved with fresh concrete,
Rumbling shadows of the freightcars tilting
        From mine to mill to guarded zone
And skies athrob with gaud and roar of firework,
        Gigantic needles jabbing high
Swiftly trailing flame like thread, then piercing
        The beady button of the moon,
Ashes on Wyoming's fodder falling,
        Milk curdled, stunted seed;

II

are we ready to go forth? Where you have come from
the students will be ever young; there it is only
the faculties and trees grow older. Leaving this friendly
hillside, you will reach your destinations—be sure
in your luggage, among trophies, clothes, and lists
of those Important Books as yet unread, to bring
the Catalogue of the Ships and tales of revolution
—the Russian, the Industrial—and explications
of both the valence table and the vertebrates
who, since the Good Duke dreamed a green world where the court
corrupts no man, agree upon hypotheses
that define the Good and tell the False from True.

III

Imperfect learning, bless this place
With possibilities of grace.
Let Mind, that ranges Heaven as far
As Barnard's pendant, lightless star,
Regard, though darkness shroud the soul,
Its constant living aureole
That casts one comprehending light
Across our chaos and the night;

Transform the deserts abstract thought
And unslaked selfishness have wrought
Into orchards where the trees
Stand rich with fruit, epitomes
Of sensuous joys that leap from birth,
Nourished in the dark of earth,
Toward sapling vigor crowned with flowers,
In acts as self-fulfilled as ours

Who build a city out of stone.
And in whose image is this done?
Defend our visionary quest,
Humane intelligence, that we
Who've eaten fruit from nature's tree
And know perfection but in art,
May, schooled and chastened by our past,
Conceive our city in the heart.

Open Letter, Returning a Questionnaire Unanswered

        —And blandish me not with the charisma
Of codex cards. I, a particular
One, a reveller irreducible in my
Republic of being, am sworn to resist
The unecstasy of the self's swift immolation
In your cold clasp of quantification.
Your multiple unchoice is irredeemable.
In none does any of my individual
Voices echo. To questions I wouldn't even ask
You mouth me answers I'd give not a syllable
Of acquiescence to. You come unbidden,
Passing beyond my identification number,
Age, sex, place of birth, to planted
Demands whose half-facts sprout five opinions
Only, excluding multiple truths. But opinions
Of half-facts are not the facts of opinion.
In the sleek city of your laws, where averages
Support constructions buttressed by totaled figures
I never come but in my ragged pocket
Carry a plot to silence the banquet speaker
And blast the foundation your fabrication stands on.
        No use to hide
In a blockhouse of filed statistics—there's no protection
In that steel box, excogitating card on card—
Well, I'm off again to my own land, scot-free,
Confiding my truths to the wind, but still on guard.

Breathing Purely

Now, at last,
I carry nothing
In my briefcase
And an empty mind.
In the meadow

Under the chestnut tree
I am a part of what I see.
Swallows above the alder thicket
Skim mosquitoes from the haze,
And I've seceded

From all committees, left
My Letters to the Editor unsent
No solutions, no opinions.
Breathing purely
Without ambitions, purged, awaiting

Annunciations of the true.
The wind is up now and the swallows gone.
I'll listen to the chestnut tree
Rustling
Empty-headed in the wind.

The Tall Maple

What waters have you sucked
Sweetening your blood
Under rough bark rising
From thin roots in the dark
As high as twigs fingering
Blazing fringes of the sun?

Your great green pavilions
Give respite from the sun's
Murderous rapacity,
Such benefits conferring
All uncaring, the late sky
Bleeding bronzed vermilions

And you standing so much taller
Than the driven creatures—
In the season of high winds
Your lithe, supple trunk bends,
All your arms toss abandoned
Leaves howling orphaned down dead ends

And now it snows on your thin bones.
The few remaining leaves
Wither on brittle withes.
Only hidden roots, suckled
By darkest rivers, can remember
Where the wild blood climbs.

Before the Fall

The impersonal sun
Pours lambent fires
Through the fusty clouds,
Through withered leaves
Oblivious of the leaves
Or of the clouds' will,
Indifferent to our desires.

On amber shafts the leaves let
Light from the zodiac lean
Against the pruned hedgerows
Ablaze upon the lawn.
Midges, nits, and gnatwings
Sink and soar. Stray winds
Transfigure some with glinting.

Poised between the Van Allen Belt
And Catherman's Drug Store,
A book is in his hand
And he may cast adrift, may soar
On shafts of light, may bring
To his feast of shadows glints of sun
Before the Fall, or withering.

The Locust

To sleep for seventeen years
In a blind bed underground
Deaf to the rant of the weather,

An idiosyncratic clock wound
To strike once, transfiguring
The dull grub, his time come round,

To be awakened fully winged,
Strong legg'd, with eyes refracting
The pitiless sun unblinkingly,

To leap glittering on the branch
And scrape rough wing on raucous thigh
In unremitting rant

Deafening the amber weather,
Then in a blind bed to plant
Dumb eggs in a nest of dirt

And lie, depleted, wrung, a withered
Carcass of silence straying ants
Will cut up against the winter

And hoard in secret tunnels
To chaw while raving weather
And stars in cold channels

Turn and turn in clockwise motion
Seventeen times full around
Till the next resurrection.

In the Cove

There was no diminishing that day.

The sun in clarity of dew arose
Toward splendors unimagined before noon.

The day kept on becoming what it was,
The hour in being what it had become.

Then nothing dwindled. Where the tide fell back
The dazzled empire of the field enlarged

And we from the cliffside to the farthest brim
Heard gulls on offshore islands calling, calling

Against the lessening of the light
And the cessation of the fields of flowers

And the tide crawling toward the darker hours
And the black fir branchtips blotting out the sky.

A waning of one stillness and a coming
Of nothing near the soughing of the trees,

Changeless, rimmed by the sea's cold sway.

Hawk Mountain

Some of us recall
Beyond town, open spaces.
You'd stride out, past the dancehall
Where the road thinned
And nobody lived, through the yarrow.
The gift's gone where that place was.

You could walk on craggy hills
That streams skirled down from
Toward marshes where the shrill
Plover skreaked. The flicker
Boomed from a tree's hollow.
Drenched earth, dazzle of air.

Night air still in the valley,
Barn swallows, cliff swallows, high
Midges on warm sun-swirls.
From that road one morning I
Turned to climb Hawk Mountain
Where south-flying hawks sail by.

On careful foot through the half-lit
Forest thickets, I heard
A sound not my sound break the ripples
Of stillness my feet had stirred:
Snapt branch: a pause: The pounding
Giddying me: Held breath—

He towered where the dark branches spread
Apart for an instant. His tread
Caressed the dead leaves. All that splendor
His dominions possessed he possessed.
His huge eyes and mine filled the silence.
The steam of his breath scared my breath—

Then he moved as a falling mountain
Carries its ridge the way down.
Two trees of his thorny wood swayed
From their roots in the suede of his crown.
At the streamside he bounded over
A great fallen pine, and was gone;

Go back to the road and follow
Over the ridges, far
Enough and you'd come to a steeple,
Graveyard, wall, galleried
Houses among shady trees
Where the days never hurried.

Where a road and one or two lanes
Converged, there lived the town.
Who throve there endured it together.
In season the feast-times came round,
Clapboard austere but fecund
The loam of the welcoming ground.

Where are those shady houses,
Where all the quiet trees?
Brisk days wheel past and the ghostly
Bitter scent of the yarrow
Fades. In Hawk Hill Gardens
Teem burrows and busy barrows.

Through skeletal thickets on chimneys
From the hill's crown you can see
From the trunk roads branch roads fork.
Give his due to the Borough Collector,
The same crop winter and summer.
Nothing untaxed can enrich us.

Banished

Tilting toward the hill with vacant frames
Webbed in windows, barn and springhouse fallen
Beneath one chestnut tree across a meadow
Gone to goldenrod and black-eyed susans—
So long unpeopled that nobody's name
Still clung like lichens to the rotting wood:
Home, this was, to a half-remembered story
Of desire denied, denied,
Of hope impossible and strange penance
Mutely lingering as the town grew round it.
Though times, though people changed, none quite forgot.
A house the wind blew through could still remind us,
A splintery house whose empty windows swung
With balls of light, aglow in summer darkness.
And if you took the steep path through the dooryard
After sledding on the far side of the hill,
Or trace of path cows may have once come down,
There'd come a sound unlike the crunch galoshes
Sink in snow with, or the runners' whoosh:
Two thumps, two thumps hard on a wooden floor,
Two thumps on wooden floor, heeltap, crutchtap
Eking a progress on a darkened stair
—Deep as your knees, snow-holes opened behind you
Till at the first lone streetlamp's civil glow
You dared to stop, shivering in brittle air,
Your hammer heart ashake—
                                        But here are houses,
Tenanted—the hill's been levelled down
Till not a trace remains. The houses here now
Show bland walls of glass to one another,

Eaveless vistas. Here the glare of newness
Blinds to losses scarcely visible
Eyes above as yet unflowered beds
And shadeless shrubs in ranks of rawness.
Late model cars crouch paired in carport stalls—
Demesne of Unpast, happy subdivision,
All grieving injured ghosts are banished hence.
If through these picture windows shifting lights
Meander on the television screens
No fear need chill the neighbor children's marrow:
Nothing left abandoned here remains
Where all that is desired can be supplied.

The Treaty

When I think of the emissaries sent us
From the tall country of the antlers
—Flint barbs fiercely glistening
And the light glinting on their feathered robes—

What was it brought them to our study?
If they'd show us
The handsigns, chalk on our ground
Those names the sun acknowledges . . .

What must we pledge ourselves to render them?

Moving among the Creatures

Moving among the creatures
As the new light
Surges down this cliff, these trees, this meadow,
Brightening the shade among the alders
And shrivelling the dew on leaves,
They are contented in their bodies—I can tell it—
The squalling gulls delighted to be turning
Widdershins, their shadows swooping
Over rocks where startled deer
Clatter, flashing spindly shanks
And delicate hooves while underfoot
Even the uglies in their sticky skins
Exult, the woodfrogs clunking all the bells
In sunken steeples, till at my
Thick tread
They leap and scissor-kick away
While the withering leech,
Shrinking, enlarging, waving
Knobbed horns
Makes the stem shine
With silver spittle where he's gone.
I trip on vines, stumble in potholes
And long for something of myself that's in them,
In the gulls' windy coursing, in the frogs'
Brief cadenza, even in the slug's
Gift to leave
A gleaming track, spun
From his own
Slippery gut.

Flocks

Flocks in Autumn flying
Past my loft
Pausing near the seven skylights
Crack open seeds on stalks that Summer
Left for some purpose,
Then whirl
Dowsing the open sky with ardent
Cries and raw cries,
Joyous disharmony,
Their flutter shading out the sun
—It was a tired sun—
And soon dart off, diminished
By distance as the swift horizon
Reaches toward them, scoops a swarm
Of dots that vanish and are still.
Silent, now
The bones of trees
Shudder in the wind. I lean and
Strain—could I shake
Free my laths from these
Joists, this plaster
Crumbling though it crack
My every pane I'd follow after
Southward before snow.

Signatures

Wings outstretched, a horned owl
Nailed beneath a crown
Of antlers on the barn door

Shrivels in the wind,
And in the swale
Among black pellets,

Signatures of deer,
The wild roses of the field
—*Rosa Virginiana*—sway

As tall as trees. Each leafy bough
Beneath the deepest center of the sky
Is scented crimson as it's green with thorns.

There, on the sky's brim, floats
One lone jet too high
To break the day's long stillnesses.

Its white breath
Splits the sky.
The halves of heaven

Are bluer than each other.
All they cover leans to sign
Bequests of their significance,

Urgent as the center of the sun,
Yet silent
And invisible

As those fixed stars
We drift beneath
In the confusions of our light.

Looking

'Windows of the soul'?
—What a view!
Looking out on slanting fields

Where clover, plantain, timothy
And stones
Stand or bend to leeward in the breezes

According to their natures,
And the trees
House chittering squirrels

Beneath the altercations of the sky
Prinked at dark
By squints of far Aldebaron;

Looking in, on nothing
But what corresponds
To this, as a swooping gull's the double

In air of that white-bellied bird
Swizzling under water
Through the upsidedown clouds swaying

Slightly in his graceful track
Where the afternoon
Has sighed and, breathing, langorously rumples

The surface of the cove with ripples
Not in the sky,
—Or is the air, for being made of sky,

A mirror that must magnify
The brute images
Cast upward by the sea?

At Evening

At evening comes a certain hour
When the teeming world remembers
It is a hostage of the dead.

Then bend in homage
The tall trees whose sprinkle of seeds
Tickled the wind. The wind is dying.

This is the hour when dust
Gleams as the tired corona leans
Its bloodied head against the rim of sky

And the dark night girds
Beyond the pulsing stars
To drop its pomps of mourning down

From windows of the houses come
Colloquial sounds and pungent odors,
Alien rhythms thrust against the night.

The Hours

It's when the afternoon is ending. Then
The hours escape their bondage to the day.

The day, depleted, weary, yearns to lay
His head upon their breasts but they

Have heard the scandal of his yen for leather,
Spurs, rigid exactions upon beds of nails

—From under ground the ravished
Shade of the morning wails—

And just because he's old now, should the hours
Be enticed? Away they stream,

Each inviolate essence still aglow.
They float upon the Milky Way like cream.

Night lays him out in dewy shroud,
Nothing accomplished shares his bed.

Far-Off Light

There are no constellations, only
Points of light
Daubed on the black slab of the night.

No gods in armor or reclining
Queens, no charismatic pizzles
On shining beasts. We do not find

Greek pictures
But trace our own creatures,
From dot to dot fill in our riddles

—Huge stallion plunges on the Milky Way
Wild eyes and nostrils rearing high
But hindlegs sunk deep in black rock

The toad that lunges from the far
Horizon, jaws apart as though to croak
Is swallowing the sky—

It almost fits into his gullet

The raging horse is nearly free.

Inviolable

Horse, huge
On the hilltop
Leaning

Massy chest
To the open sky,
Unhaltered sun,

Meadows and
The hankering sea
Embracing—

O great
Creatures I would clasp
And nuzzle

Over the barbed
Wire fence
Though I trespass

My boundaries,
Breaking
Your laws.

A Bringing of Bread, 1928

The baker's waggon rumbles down the street
In chariot splendor
Announced by horseshoes' clang on stone

And a sweetness in the air.
Only bread brings
Such halcyon shifts upon the dooryard breezes.

When he dismounts the baker is benign.
A giant bearing
Trays of loaves

Pats the high rump of the horse
Who whinnies in his nosebag.
He leaves the kitchen richer when he leaves,

And steeped molasses and the toasted
Scent of sugar and of yeast
From crullers, doughnuts, loaves, unrolls

Around the bannisters and through the windows.
He's off now on his other calls,
And in the street a squall of sparrows

Excavates the golden grains
From steaming windfalls. Sweeter
The morning where the baker's waggon rolls.

A Solitary

Oblique essence of the personal,
Your individuality's a hanged man on the neck
Of an albatross. O let the bird fly free,

That wide-winged soul has never
Shot a quill at you,
Murderer of your double!

Lacking companion, now
Exulting that you are unique,
You stake your camp on spiritual territory,

Not the human. Self-contemplation
Must be the range of your philosophy,
O bleak essence of the personal.

The Companion

Whether we come, in last imaginings,
To our earliest unremembered dream,
Or at the end it's still discovery,
Always the conquest of a final shore,

He will be waiting for me there,
As ever second-sighted and first there:
I groping my way in radiant day,
He cleaving midnight quick as flame;

He owns my features, favored gaunt as I,
Good luck's all his, yet he takes mine with me.
My tedious failures he disowns,
No place I triumph but it is his home.

The Last Arrival

The last arrival in the furthest country,
All he saw he saw as mystery.
He to doorknob, counterpane and incised stone
That chanced to notice him appeared
Too familiar for comment.

And so they got used to one another,
The mysteries and the familiar.
In time all mysteries became familiars.
He in long familiarity
Disowned their secrets of their mystery.

Ceasing to notice him, they left as though
By prearrangement for the nearest country.
Someone will be the first to find that country,
In reciprocity for its reality
Will learn new names of all the mysteries

And write such full particulars in letters home
Unlike all correspondence known,
Since he with counterpane, doorknob and cut stone
Will parse that language of their own
To blurt out mysteries in ours, where all's familiar.

'He was the first who had returned'

He was the first who had returned
From that country
Of another tongue.

Speech, there,
Used purer forms of ecstasy than love
Here. Our actions fumble
With a gross vocabulary.

He makes the world
Around him glow
In simplicity of light.
His nouns are proverbs but their wisdom lies

Useless
In our boroughs of necessity,
Pure homage
Only known
When blood has crumpled, all its glories gone.

'When my wiser brother'

When my wiser brother
Who speaks so rarely
And only in my voice

(He is too busy matching souls
To the trees they will resemble, lovers
With one another,
The seahorse and the sun,
Sweet labor,
There's little time for speech)—when he

Finds words
Acceptable I will declare him,
For I am ready:
My phonemes, signs, parentheses
Await his spell.

All will be well
Disposed to consecrate the map
Of new peninsulas he will bequeath me.
But just when I've stepped out to choose the wine
For the banquet of our fond reunion
He will be gone,
Off to that republic
Of pure possibility
Where he plots a *coup d'état* against my exile.
Sometime, he may reveal it,

Though I am left meanwhile
Unbrothered,
My words all fled from split cicada skins
Into a busy fraction of the day.

The Way He Went

He didn't go away
To the roll of drums
Or to annunciatory thunder
Of mantic voices,

He didn't leave by the long light
Of line-storms slashing doomed horizons
Or the guiding blink and dousing
Of little harbor lights,

He went by darkness and by daylight going
A silent way
Vacating endless
Acreages of parking-lots and marshes

Still
Then evening all atwitch with raucous birds
Ignorant of the emptiness that fell
Lighter than dew.

He went
And the stars shone hard and rocks
Arose in their accustomed risings
From the sea while broken clouds

Scudded around and closed against
Ragged towers of a city
Gathering tumults of electric signboards
Glowing in the sky where many colors

Made one color
As before.

The Hero

1. The Path

Another forking of the road, and he
Must take one way, closing forever other
Untouched splendors not to be achieved.

At his journey's setting-out all doorways
Leaned toward possibility. He strode
Onward, toward the gleams of distant roads.

Now gates are barred.
Among those broken paths there is but one
His blade may clear by toil of many blows,

One track, faint in the snow, further from succor.
There, above the winks of hostel lights
The destination that he chose awaits him.

2. Onward

Onward his journey led
Up the mountain.
Travelling light, accustoming
His breath to thinner air;

At last, a sense he was approaching where
He had been meant to go—
Then, just as he'd mastered climbing
The path led
Down.

3. *The Victor*

When the fight was over
And the enemy lay dead
The victor shuddered in a daze,
Holding the butchered head

Of one whose strength had all but matched his strength,
Whose wile he undid by his guile.
Proven, his own superiority.
Still he quakes, tasting in victory

Blood hated, yet prized.
He had put on
That murderous character, in foe despised,
And how suck air in innocence again?

4. *The Return*

When he came, after initiation
—The sufferings, the temptation—
To that dread place
Of undoing,

Hazarding mortality in the one
Gesture of a hero,
And at his feet the rock shard
And in his hand the sword,

How could he know
He must discover now
A new fellowship,
Since men

With fear and women in delight
Will seek renown
By strife to bind his fierce arms
And famous heart;

Where find the foe or friend
Or lover who would own
Him for the man he was before that blow
Set him apart?

First Flight

I watches me climb
in the cockpit, him fixing
the belt and waving
my hand I see

the prop rev and the plane
cough forward
both winds biting
sudden wind

I on ground invisible
sees me taxi obvious
behind him Wild Pilot
what I doing there & here

particularly when
up high he says
Dan,
he says, Dan boy,

take over I don't feel
too good after all
that Scotch-type rot
last night I'm flying

me at the joystick o
boy how come
those chickens getting bigger chasing
their shadows under stoops

I see it clearly
clearly
STICK BACK!
and we climb

higher than the sun
sinking in a stew of clouds
Well Major anything
for a laugh me say

I says let's bring her down

Creature

Sidles from a fissure in the mind,
Flings upon the foetid air
Elbows that claw and flail,
Then flings wide its beak
As though from the fissure of that craw the shriek
Could split those walls
And guileless air
On burst of sun or echoed beam
Of moon break in upon
The echo of this scream
That calls and calls and calls and sprawls
Sunk deep below the reach
Of breath assuaged by moon or sun
Or the release of speech.

Lines for Jack Clemo

author of *The Map of Clay*,
now blind and deaf,
a 'Prisoner of God'

I stand on gritty Goonamarris,
The four elements assail me.
How can my senses hold all Nature's
Clarity and the soil of man?

He, leonine before the firescreen, paces
The kingdom of deprivation's borders
Striking the stones to make them sing.
No land's so bleak he cannot find those stones:

His Adversary guards the glazed ground.
They wrestle head to head and wound to wound,
Then inward darkness burns away,
Shards of silence frame the essential psalm.

The Wastrel

This blear-eyed sun
Lurches down the horizon's
Street, deserted, cold.
He is himself the dull

Penny he beseeches.
Will no one help to fill
His empty cup?
Who'd think his gaze was golden

When he mounted up
The morning's tower of glass—
Then poised at the very top,
Profligate in air,

It was himself that made
What's paltry or despised
Resemble him. Each blade
Of grass he swathed in grace,

Dust blessed him to his face.
Dung shone in benison.
Who could forget that noon!
Yet who brings him its light

Now that his battered head
Totters down the road,
Or will repay the debt
Owed to spent delight?

Keys

As the days grow shorter many keys
Hang from our chains—
Keys to boxes, drawers, trunks, and rooms
Filled with trunks and drawers
And boxes, keys to vaults and keys to houses,
Heavy keys of wrought-iron, filed
To fit the doors we can't remember closing.
Keys that seem unlike our own
Keys that we would open gates with.
Walking through the aery corridors and gates
Ever ajar,
The road ahead unbarred and open
—See, if we turn
Around, the way lies
Behind us. We could go
Back down the very lanes we've been
Where nothing's changed,
Had we the one
Key that doesn't
Hang from these heavy chains.

Entering Doorways

Entering doorways
Exchanging rooms
The last room leaving
Lost words ringing
In the head clinging
Seeking silence
The silence clanging
This side the threshhold
Snatches of old talk
Entering doorways.

Exchanging rooms
A room once entered
Invades the new space
These doors where the doors were
Old chests in their place
Chairs where the chairs were
Wind in the fireplace
Bed in the bed place
Voices and faces
Recurrent in strangeness
And in this new room
Enmeshed in these traces
Strain toward the doorway
To the next room
Entering doorways
Exchanging rooms.

The Summerhouse

Climbed uphill to the seashore summerhouse,
Domed and shingled cottage occupied
By certain predecessors in whose pots
Our porridge bubbles merrily. The waves
Crash beyond the windows. Without ceremony
They pack their things and are about to go.
Well, we will soon forget them walking
Dourly without shadows two by two.
It's our vacation, sheets dried in the sun—
Out from the floorboard, underneath the bed
With slightest scrape of scale on wooden grain
The flattened head of a silent copperhead
—A kitchen cleaver leaps into my hand,
Shining through the high song of your fear
The whacking silver arc of light descends
And head rolls, chomping, and the lithe
And lovely diamonds down the back writhe.
He, he, tall, returns, removes
A curved and grooved tooth and squeezes it
Into my palm. —'Here, it's yours now.'—'Thanks,
But might I not, as a memento, keep
The head?'—'Oh no, there's poison in the fangs.'
And now he's dropped the snake into his thermos
Of iced tea ('The place is yours') and driven
Down the sinuous twisting distant road.
And we've the sunny, salty, freshened air
And wind-dried linen sheets to spread.

In the Republic of the Troll King

In the Republic of the Troll King
The page-boy or the Minister
Could not be sure
Was he perhaps the Jester?
Or Seneschal a Troubadour

Singing how in his cage of bones
The lover sang to the lady leaning
From crenelated tower,
In hopes to sweeten the still air
That breathed around her;

Standing behind the King, who dozed
Nor saw the hooded horseman coming.
The freedom of the palace
Is granted none but who will trace
Its inner and most secret place.

Sceptre and bells he bears forthwith
In gaiety, in dignity;
The bridge is drawn
That crossers of the moat strode on,
In fact the bridge is gone,

In truth the palace is a keep,
The stairs up that whorled tower steep,
The lady leaning
And the hawk hung from the sky asleep
And his careening

Rush of breath blasts through the halls,
Gutters the candles on the walls,
And now he takes her.
The hawk upon the horseman falls.
His sceptre wakes her,

And her long hair twines down her shoulder
And her long arms entangle him,
Him she crowns.
And in the freedom of that place
They smilingly come down.

The Tale-Teller

Imagining a Father
Telescoped by time and distance nearer,
Larger, sitting at the bed's edge
—Beyond the sill the humpbacked branches
Conspire in cloaks; the gasping moon
Mints shadows on a desert floor—
But then the third wish of the seventh son,
A spindly cowherd with a knee of kibes
Who wears his good luck like a warm great-coat,
Flings open all the dormers and the night breathes
Companionable fragrance of new bread.
Branches flutter bannerets of birdsong.
The raggedy goosegirl claims her minion now
In golden gown and crown and silver shawl,
In all that empire theirs the one true fiefdom. All
That glowed between the grassblades and the moon
Grew luminous with love that spilled from them.
That's how the story ends. They loved each other
And their love like dew rejoiced the kingdom
And the teller of their tale
Was larger, nearer,
And his word was real.

Another Country

Coming to a cavern in a valley,
Who would not explore?
His pineknot lit, he thrust a way
Past droppings on the mossy floor,
Past walls that gleamed and streamed with waters
Into a chamber none had known before
 Save who drew in colors deep as blood
The great creatures on that sacred dome
—Horned Huntsman, and the Woman, Moon—
It was then he found the doorway
To another country. Darkness
There is brighter than familiar noon.
The light that lights that land's like lightning
Its sudden crackle rends the skies.
                                        He tries
To tell a prospect of that country,
His words as much like lightning as the mutter
Of seared cloud
When the bolt's dazzle has come, and gone.

Musebaby

Who put a mackintosh around
Venus of the Louvre? The pensive tilt
Of head, that hidden half a smile as though
Remembering a secret, and the downward
Sloping of the rounded shoulders—Yes, it was
On the Boulevard Raspail, when
From the Metro
You stepped, astonishing the day.

'It cannot come because desired'

It cannot come because desired,
It makes
Its own weather, its own time
Glowing
Like the phosphorescent wake
Of ships,
Mysterious tumult
Slitting the sensuous sea.

Love does not know
How we retrace
Together our most desperate seeking
Our most sacred place;

It's with these
Banal bodies
That we must
Make do,
Their strangely bulged and cherished
Curvatures, their folds, their flanks,
Their impermanent
Ageing surfaces
Concealing

Messages that we
Discover, each
The other's own
Rosetta Stone—

Love, I never hear
The brusque unpurposed clamor of the street
Or breathe the damp
Dolor that floods our city from the vast
Cool vats of space
But hold, an amulet against mischance,
Remembrance of your touch,
Your hands, your urgent hips,
The imperishable light, your sleeping face.

'Ignorant of source'

Ignorant of source,
Of consequence,
Love does not know
Its cause, its end,

Instinctually goes
About its business, opening
For a dozen minutes, maybe more,
The almost unendurable
Delight before
The closing once again
Of its blazing door.

Last night it opened as it had
Fifteen years ago.
That supersensual light
Made me father then,
And now we know
It's on our Father's errand
That we come and go.

Lovers into parents, we
Were transformed by love
Yet are the same.
Those who deeply think have said
That by the action of
A divine Love
The Unmoved Mover made the world.
Ever unchanged,
He must be changed thereby, begetting

New loves, new
Ways of loving, being loved.
Such reciprocities
Between what love creates and love
Were unforetold.
How could He know
His children would become the world?

Last Words

Eleven o'clock. It's time
I made my will. To you,
Musebaby, I leave
These jottings.

What will you do with them?

They are of no earthly use,
And you deserve, require
A goodly world of looking-after—
I'd fit you out

With the whole kit and garterbelt,
Gowns, togas, suits, capote,
Any hat you choose; a house
With miracle kitchen, an antique

Butcher's table, and perfume,
Bath-oil, a carved four-poster
With a featherbed and tester,
A daughter and a son,

Life insurance, car—the lot.
It's a life I'd give you.
How can I leave it with you?
Where go without you?

That would be nowhere, no life,
Nothing like the bits and pieces
Of the life that's in these scribblings
I make because of you,

Though little good they do you.
You don't care, you needn't.
You are yourself, it's you I need
And all I leave are but the ways

I've found of saying so.

A Marriage

'Remember that farmer down in Maine
Who said to us, "I've been
An abandoned island
Since she's gone"?

—That's the hurt of proud flesh
We've known,
The heart's self-borne contagion
When you or I have parted us

With those rending, furious
Irretrievable accusations.
Each gulp of air keeps the wound fresh.
Left to the individual freedom

Of broken ends
We can't make meet, I roar
Off, a space-bound satellite
With no earth to encircle, adrift

In that unfinished void
Where nothing numbs the red scar
Of a burnt-out asteroid.
And yet I turn, seeking some tremor

Of your light,
Your heat,
Wherever in that emptiness
You are.'

This Life

This life, this
Distracted city
Beyond this garden and

Ourselves when we
Most clearly see
Ourselves: all, figures moving

Mirrored under water—
Imagine our originals!
—Fed by what they feed,

The vivid light of pure
Energy. The he
Of whom I am the blur

Moves toward only her
Whom you most resemble. Love,
We plunge

Upward toward each other
Like salmon drowning
In bright air, and fall

Renewed in this
Common stream, our own
Illusory element.

'Who was it came'

Who was it came
Over the mountains bearing
Gifts we did not ask?

—Not the sapience of the thrush
Or the ant's perdurance,
Something a body might use—

Who was it brought
Cerements and a wrinkled skin,
A sour digestion

Over the mountains, offering
Crotchets and a rheumy gaze
And wits gone wandering?

Just when we thought to repossess
The taut frenzies of Chicago jazz
And bridal ardor

Here he comes,
Inexorable gaffer in an old hat
Croaking our names.

Another Border

Was it we who stumbled
Unawares across a border
Into a bleaker diocese,

Or did October's camouflage
Of crisp and primal colors
Infiltrate the parish of our pleasures?

No matter now
Who crossed whom, these colder
Wizened days that crowd us

And you and I
Thrusting impatient through their shorter
Gaps of lessened light

Move forward
Toward another border
—It must be there

Awaiting us,
That apostolic territory
To which we go.